HOW TO DRAW
WONDER WOMAN,
GREEN LANTERN,

AND OTHER
DC SUPER HEROES

by Aaron Sautter

illustrated by Tim Levins

Wonder Woman created by William Moulton Marston

CAPSTONE PRESS
a capstone imprint

Published in 2015 by Capstone Press,
a Capstone Imprint
1710 Roe Crest Drive
North Mankato, Minnesota 56003
www.capstonepub.com

STAR33521

Library of Congress Cataloging-in-Publication Data
Sautter, Aaron.
How to draw Wonder Woman, Green Lantern, and other DC super heroes /
by Aaron Sautter, illustrated by Tim Levins.
pages cm.—(DC Super heroes. Drawing DC super heroes)
Summary: "Simple step-by-step instructions teach readers how to draw Wonder Woman,
Green Lantern, The Flash, and several other DC super heroes"—Provided by publisher.
ISBN 978-1-4914-2154-3 (library binding)
1. Cartoon characters—Juvenile literature. 2. Superheroes in art—Juvenile literature.
3. Drawing—Technique—Juvenile literature. I. Title.
NC1764.8.H47S288 2015
741.5'1—dc23   2014023864

Credits
Designer: Ted Williams
Art Director: Nathan Gassman
Production Specialist: Kathy McColley

Design Elements
Capstone Studio: Karon Dubke; Shutterstock: Artishok, Bennyartist, Eliks, Mazzzur, Roobcio

Printed in the United States of America in North Mankato, Minnesota.
092014   008482CGS15

0 1021 0292088 5

DRAWING PROJECTS

LET'S DRAW AMAZING DC SUPER HEROES! 4

WHAT YOU'LL NEED 5

WONDER WOMAN 7

GREEN LANTERN 8

THE FLASH 11

GREEN ARROW 13

AQUAMAN 15

MARTIAN MANHUNTER 16

CYBORG 18

BLACK CANARY 20

SHAZAM! 23

SUPERGIRL 25

NIGHTWING 27

THE JUSTICE LEAGUE 28

INTERNET SITES 32

LET'S DRAW AMAZING DC SUPER HEROES!

Superman and Batman aren't the only super heroes fighting the forces of evil. Wonder Woman, Green Lantern, The Flash, Supergirl, and many other super heroes work just as hard to stop super-villains' wicked plans. Super heroes come from a wide range of backgrounds and have many different powers. Some are human. Others come from alien worlds. Some heroes had loving families as kids, while others grew up as orphans. Some were born with their abilities. Others got their powers accidentally or received them as gifts. However, as different as they are, super heroes all have one thing in common. They all have a strong desire to fight for justice and protect innocent people.

Welcome to the world of DC Super Heroes! On the following pages you'll learn to draw Wonder Woman, Green Lantern, Cyborg, and several other incredible heroes.

Use the power of your imagination to send your favorite super heroes on new awesome adventures!

WHAT YOU'LL NEED

You don't need superpowers to draw mighty heroes. But you'll need some basic tools. Gather the following supplies before starting your awesome art.

PAPER: You can get special drawing paper from art supply and hobby stores. But any type of blank, unlined paper will work fine.

PENCILS: Drawings should always be done in pencil first. Even the pros use them. If you make a mistake, it'll be easy to erase and redo it. Keep plenty of these essential drawing tools on hand.

PENCIL SHARPENER: To make clean lines, you need to keep your pencils sharp. Get a good pencil sharpener. You'll use it a lot.

ERASERS: As you draw, you're sure to make mistakes. Erasers give artists the power to turn back time and erase those mistakes. Get some high quality rubber or kneaded erasers. They'll last a lot longer than pencil erasers.

BLACK MARKER PENS: When your drawing is ready, trace over the final lines with black marker pen. The dark lines will help make your characters stand out on the page.

COLORED PENCILS AND MARKERS: Ready to finish your masterpiece? Bring your characters to life and give them some color with colored pencils or markers.

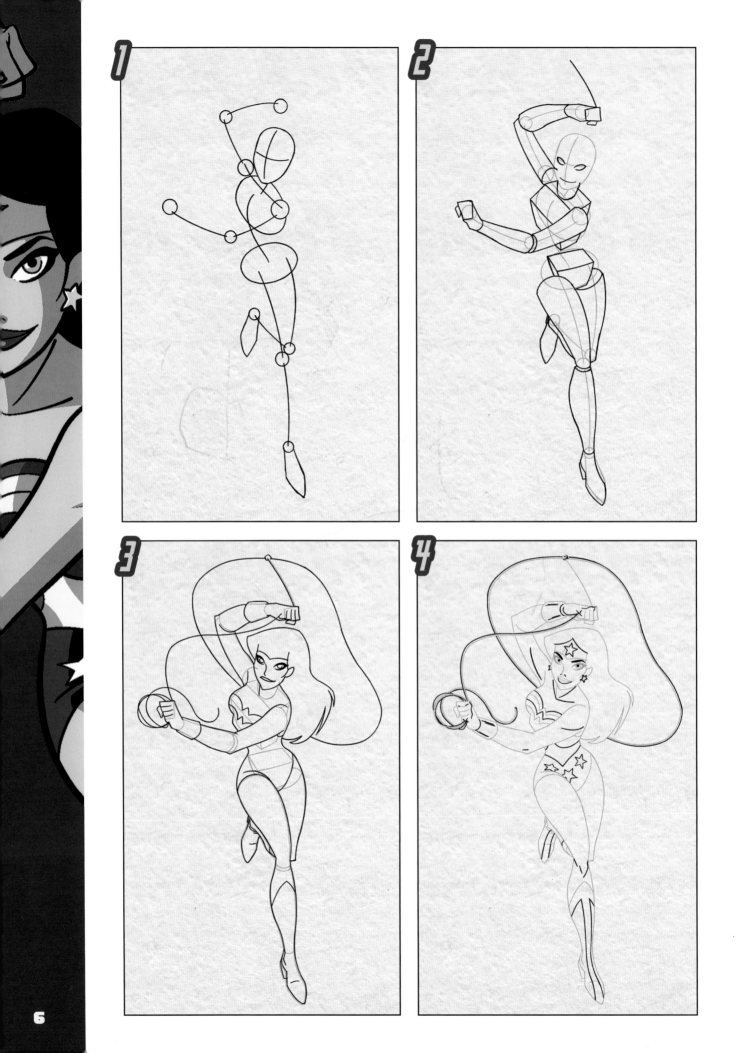

DRAWING IDEA
Try drawing Wonder Woman battling her archenemy Cheetah!

WONDER WOMAN

Real Name: Princess Diana

Home Base: Island of Themyscira

Occupation: Amazon princess, crime fighter

Abilities: super-strength and speed, flight

Equipment: indestructible bracelets, magical tiara, Lasso of Truth

Background: Diana is the Princess of Themyscira, the hidden home of the Amazons. But as she grew up, Diana knew she could be more than just an Amazonian princess. She trained hard and became highly skilled in hand-to-hand combat. Now, with her magical tiara, indestructible bracelets, and Lasso of Truth, Diana fights the forces of evil as Wonder Woman.

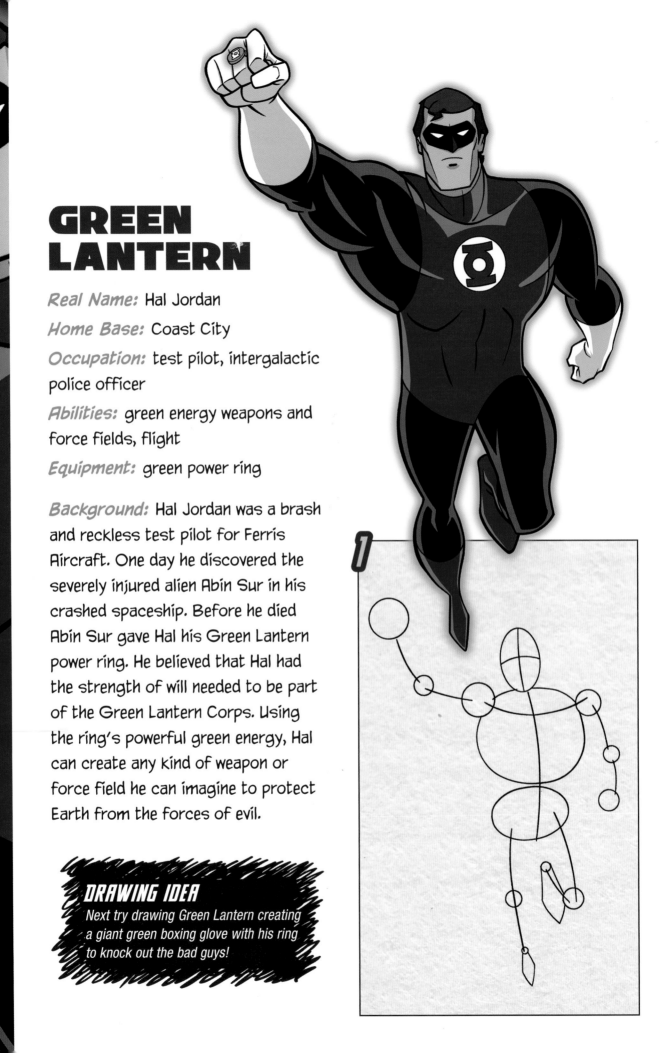

GREEN LANTERN

Real Name: Hal Jordan

Home Base: Coast City

Occupation: test pilot, intergalactic police officer

Abilities: green energy weapons and force fields, flight

Equipment: green power ring

Background: Hal Jordan was a brash and reckless test pilot for Ferris Aircraft. One day he discovered the severely injured alien Abin Sur in his crashed spaceship. Before he died Abin Sur gave Hal his Green Lantern power ring. He believed that Hal had the strength of will needed to be part of the Green Lantern Corps. Using the ring's powerful green energy, Hal can create any kind of weapon or force field he can imagine to protect Earth from the forces of evil.

DRAWING IDEA
Next try drawing Green Lantern creating a giant green boxing glove with his ring to knock out the bad guys!

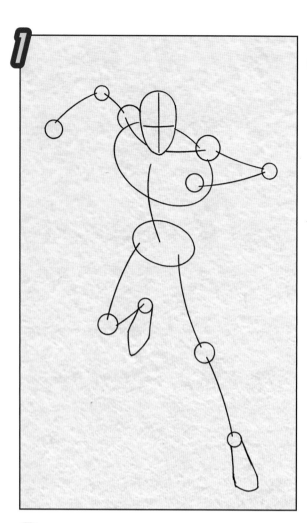

5

DRAWING IDEA
Try drawing The Flash
outrunning the icy rays
from Captain Cold's gun!

THE FLASH

Real Name: Barry Allen

Home Base: Central City

Occupation: forensic scientist, crime fighter

Abilities: super-speed, accelerated healing, phasing

Background: Forensic scientist Barry Allen was working in his lab one stormy night when a powerful bolt of lightning shot through a window. The lightning destroyed a chemical cabinet, soaking Barry in electrified chemicals. Shortly after the accident Barry discovered he could move at supersonic speeds. He can even vibrate his body so fast that he can phase right through solid walls! As The Flash, Barry uses his super speed to save people in danger and stop criminals in their tracks.

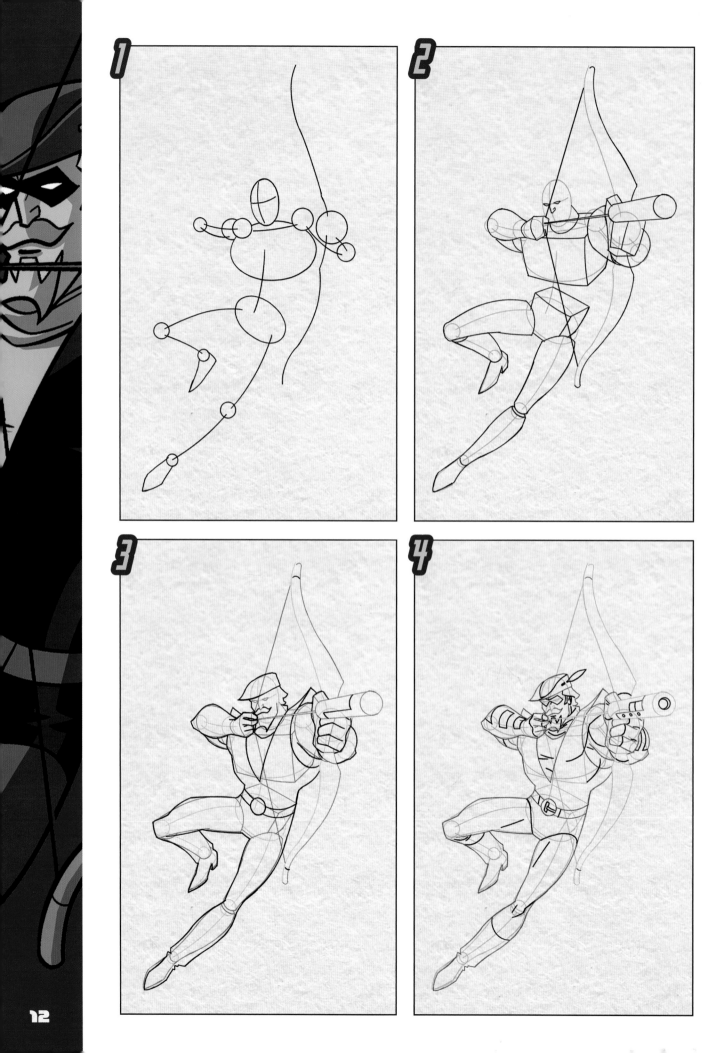

5

DRAWING IDEA
Next try drawing Green Arrow
using his trick arrows to stop
a criminal's getaway car!

GREEN ARROW

Real Name: Oliver "Ollie" Queen

Home Base: Star City

Occupation: billionaire businessman
and politician, crime fighter

Abilities: expert marksmanship,
hand-to-hand combat skills

Equipment: trick arrows

Background: As a boy Oliver
Queen was skilled with a bow,
and his hero was Robin Hood.
When Ollie's parents were killed,
he grew into a rich and spoiled
thrill-seeker who cared only for
himself. But that all changed one
day when he was stranded on a
small island. There he learned to
survive by honing his fighting skills
and becoming a master archer.
After being rescued Oliver decided
to change his ways. He now models
himself after his childhood hero.
He dresses in green and uses his
amazing archery skills to keep
crime off the streets of Star City.

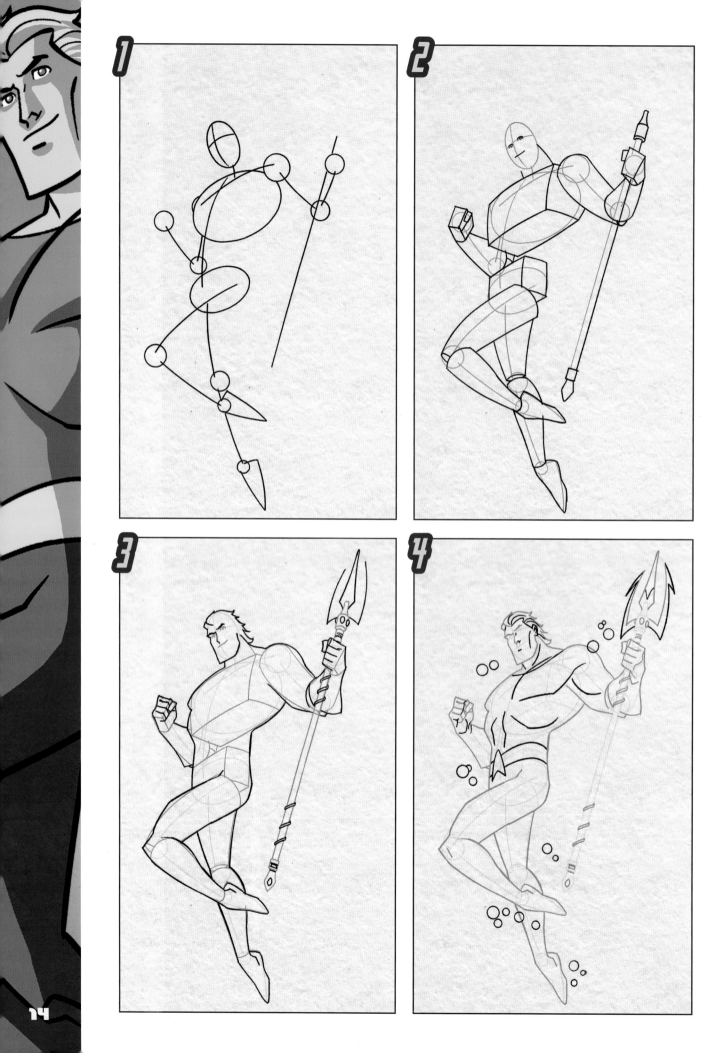

DRAWING IDEA
Try drawing Aquaman communicating with some sea creatures to stop Black Manta's evil plans!

AQUAMAN

Real Name: Arthur Curry

Home Base: Atlantis

Occupation: King of Atlantis, protector of the oceans

Abilities: super-strength and speed, underwater breathing, telepathic communication

Background: Arthur Curry grew up as the son of a lighthouse keeper. At a young age, Arthur learned he could breathe underwater and talk to fish and other ocean animals. Eventually Arthur learned that his mother was the Queen of Atlantis and that he would one day be a king. When he grew up, Arthur decided to use his powers to defend the Earth's oceans and wildlife and help stop the world's worst villains.

1

DRAWING IDEA
Next try drawing J'onn J'onzz taking
the shape of a powerful animal to
help Green Lantern defeat Sinestro!

MARTIAN MANHUNTER

Real Name: J'onn J'onzz

Home Base: Mars, Justice League Watchtower

Occupation: detective, Martian police officer

Abilities: super-strength and speed, flight, telepathy,
shape-shifting, investigation

Background: When powerful aliens invaded Mars, the Martian race was nearly
wiped out. As the last survivor, J'onn J'onzz managed to escape and fled
to Earth. There he joined Earth's mightiest heroes to defeat the alien threat.
Afterward J'onn decided to make Earth his new home. Using his shape-shifting
ability, J'onn blends in with Earth's people. He uses his telepathic powers and
detective skills to solve crimes and stop villains' wicked plans.

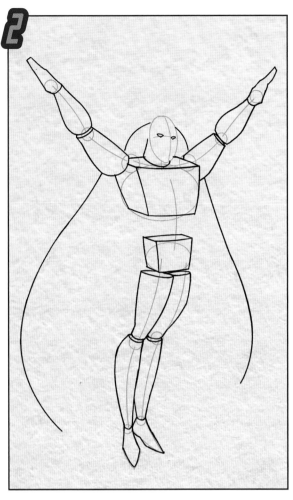

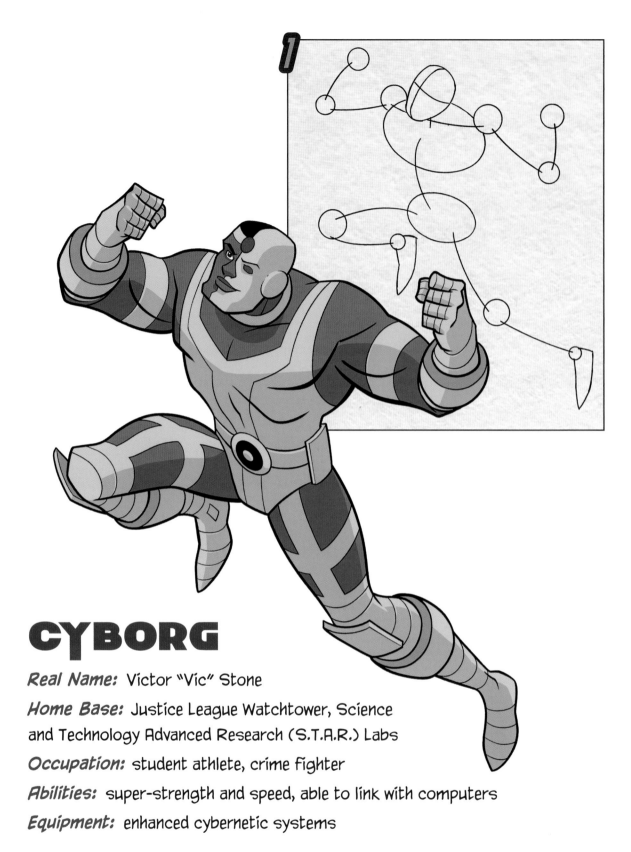

CYBORG

Real Name: Victor "Vic" Stone

Home Base: Justice League Watchtower, Science and Technology Advanced Research (S.T.A.R.) Labs

Occupation: student athlete, crime fighter

Abilities: super-strength and speed, able to link with computers

Equipment: enhanced cybernetic systems

Background: Victor "Vic" Stone was visiting his father at the local S.T.A.R. Lab when he was horribly injured in an accident. Vic's father saved his life by replacing much of his body with cybernetic parts. Vic's new body gives him superhuman abilities, and he can link with almost any computer in the world. Vic once dreamed of becoming a star athlete. But now he has a new purpose—to fight crime as one of the world's greatest heroes.

DRAWING IDEA
Try drawing Cyborg lifting a smashed car to save someone trapped underneath it.

19

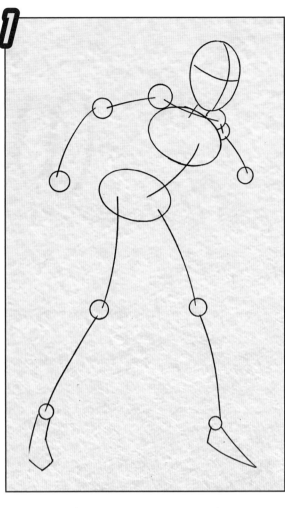

DRAWING IDEA
Next draw Black Canary using her special ability to help Green Arrow stop a bank robbery!

BLACK CANARY

Real Name: Dinah Lance

Home Base: Gotham City

Occupation: adventurer, crime fighter

Abilities: martial arts expert, ultrasonic "Canary Cry" scream

Background: Dinah Lance comes from a family of crime fighters. Her father is a police officer, and her mother fought crime as the original Black Canary. Her mother didn't want her to become a crime fighter, but Dinah followed in her mother's footsteps anyway. However, Dinah has a special ability of her own. Her ultrasonic "Canary Cry" scream can stun foes, damage objects, and even shatter metal!

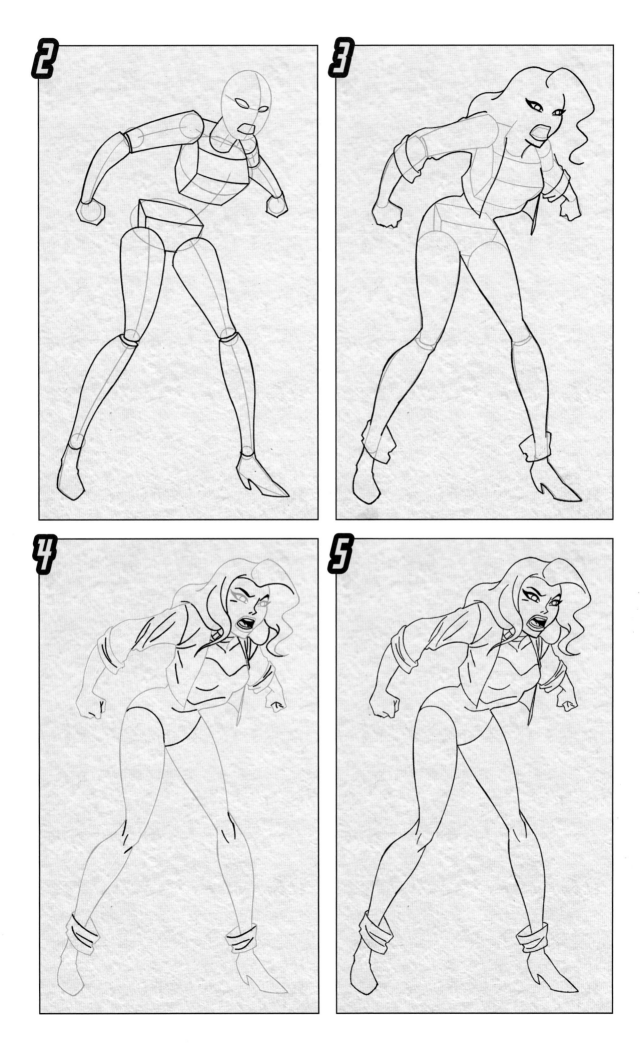

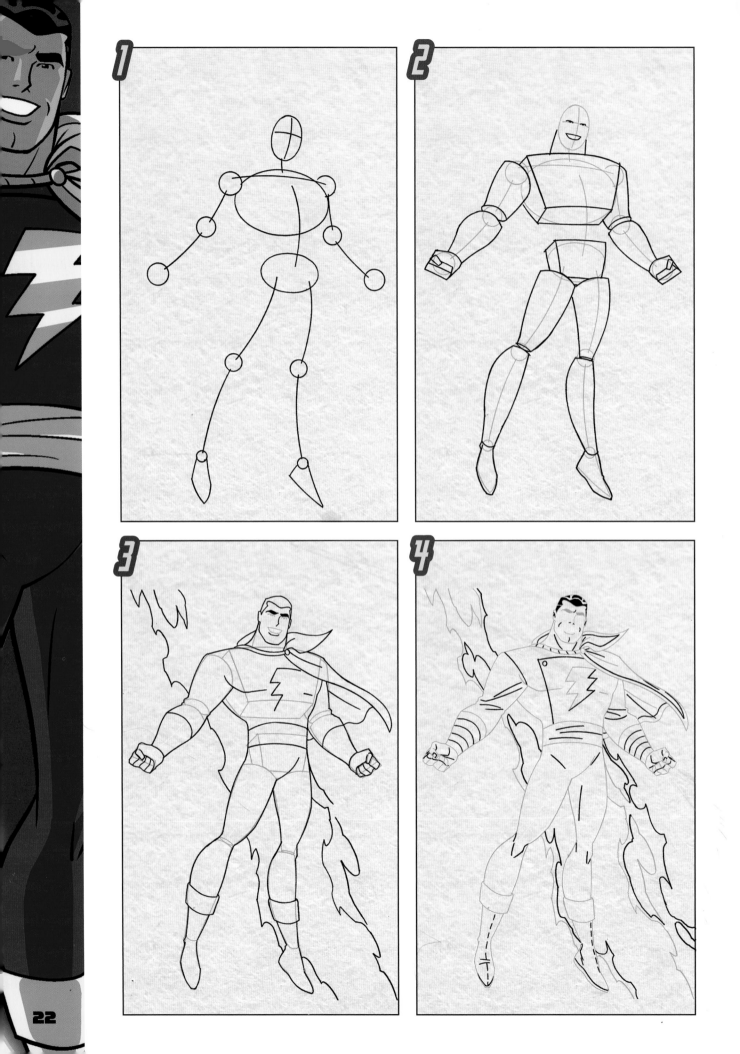

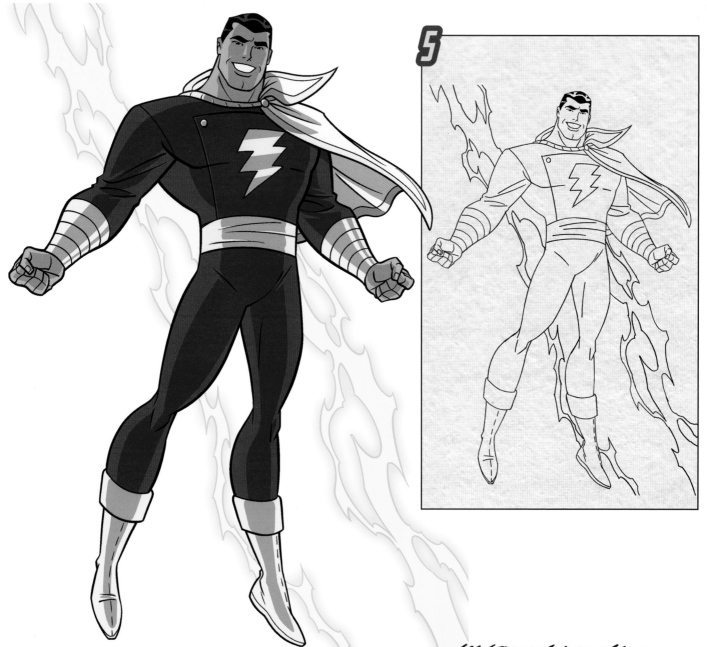

SHAZAM!

Real Name: William "Billy" Batson

Home Base: Fawcett City

Occupation: student, reporter, super hero

Abilities: super-strength, speed, and stamina; flight; invulnerability

Background: Young Billy Batson's parents were killed during an archaeology expedition in Egypt. The powerful wizard Shazam! soon learned about Billy and his strong sense of justice. The wizard gave Billy the powers of several historical figures. These include the wisdom of Solomon, the strength of Hercules, the stamina of Atlas, the power of Zeus, the courage of Achilles, and the speed of Mercury. Now when Billy calls out the magic word "SHAZAM!," he is transformed into a mighty hero who is almost as powerful as Superman!

DRAWING IDEA
Try drawing SHAZAM! fighting his archenemy Black Adam to stop him from taking over the world!

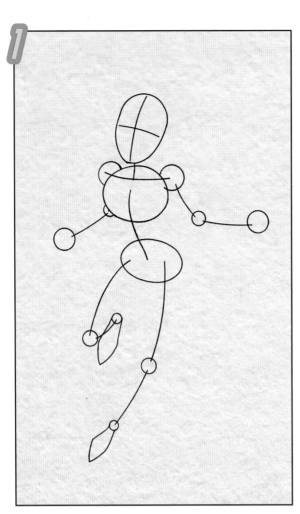

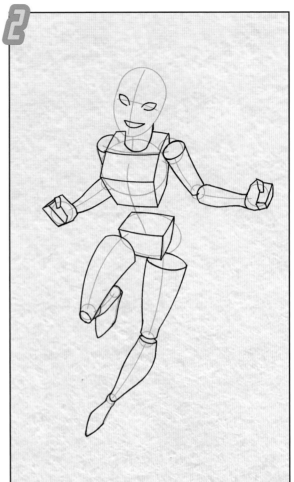

5

DRAWING IDEA

Try drawing Supergirl fighting along with Superman to stop Brainiac from destroying Earth!

SUPERGIRL

Real Name: Kara Zor-El

Home Base: Metropolis

Occupation: student, super hero

Abilities: super-strength, speed, and hearing; X-ray vision; heat vision; flight; invulnerability

Background: Kara Zor-El is Superman's cousin and the last survivor of Krypton's Argo City. Like Kal-El, Kara was sent to Earth in a spacecraft. Superman took Kara to live with the Kents as their teenage niece. The Kents taught her the same values they had taught Clark. Meanwhile, Superman taught her how to control her newfound abilities. Eventually Kara moved to Metropolis to fight crime as Supergirl.

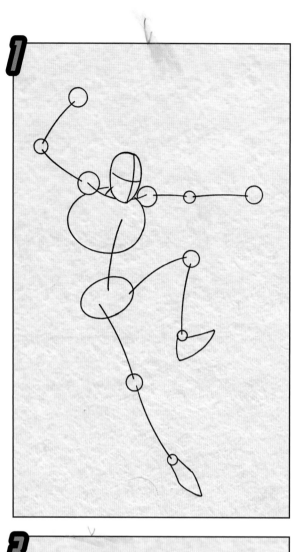

DRAWING IDEA
Now try drawing Nightwing using his acrobatic skills to take out a group of thugs on the street!

NIGHTWING

Real Name: Dick Grayson

Home Base: Blüdhaven

Occupation: adventurer, crime fighter

Abilities: master of martial arts and acrobatics, master detective

Equipment: pair of fighting sticks

Background: As a boy Dick Grayson was a member of the Flying Graysons, a family of circus acrobats. When Dick's parents were killed in a tragic accident, Bruce Wayne took in the heartbroken boy. When Dick learned that Bruce was secretly Batman, he began training to become the first Robin. Batman and Robin spent several years fighting crime together as the Dynamic Duo. But when Dick grew up, he struck out on his own. He created a new suit for himself and moved to a new city. Now he protects the streets of Blüdhaven as the acrobatic crime fighter, Nightwing.

THE JUSTICE LEAGUE

When Earth was invaded by powerful aliens, even the world's mightiest heroes were unable to defeat them on their own. Only by joining together did they have the strength to overcome the alien threat. After stopping the invasion, Superman, Batman, Wonder Woman, Green Lantern, The Flash, and Martian Manhunter formed the Justice League. The heroes then built the Watchtower, a space station that orbits the Earth. From here the Justice League can watch over Earth and launch powerful defenses to protect its people.

1

2

INTERNET SITES

FactHound offers a safe, fun way to find Internet sites related to this book.
All of the sites on FactHound have been researched by our staff.

Here's all you do:

Visit www.facthound.com

Type in this code: 9781491421543

 Check out projects, games and lots more at
www.capstonekids.com

TITLES IN THIS SET

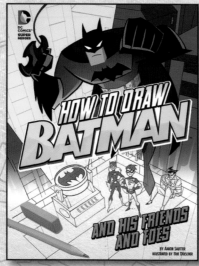